David the Daydreamer

Written by Nick Beare and Jeanette Greenwell

Illustrated by Paula Martyr

David the Daydreamer	page	2
What are you good at?	page	20
Activities	page	24
Word List	page	30

David the Daydreamer

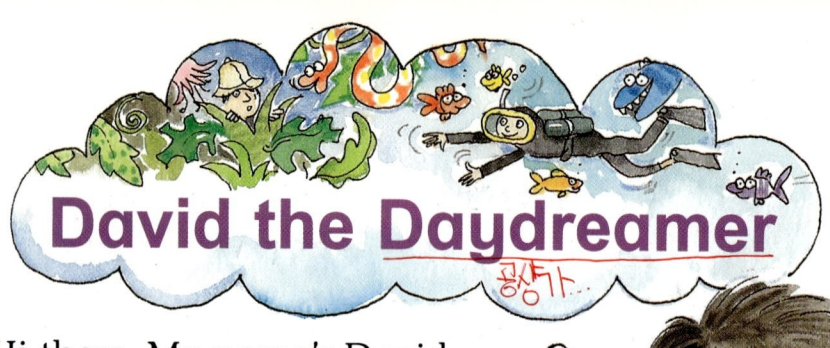

Hi there. My name's David. I live with my mother, my father, and my brother in a small town. My family are very special people.

First, I'm going to tell you about my father. My father is an inventor. He makes amazing machines.

One machine makes your bed in the morning. Another machine takes your dog for a walk and another machine cooks your lunch for you.

Yes, my father is a very special person.

2

Next, I'm going to tell you about my mother. She's a musician. She plays the piano. She gives concerts and lots of people go to hear her play the piano. This is what people do at the end of her concerts: They clap for a long time. They throw flowers on the stage. They ask for her autograph.

I'm very proud of my mother. She's a very special person.

And this is my brother. He has a computer. He works on his computer all day. He knows everything about computers. This is what he can do with his computer: He can write music. He can make cartoon figures. He can make amazing patterns. He can do very difficult things on his computer.

He says it's easy! My brother is a very clever person.

And finally, there's me. I can't invent machines. I can't play the piano. I don't understand computers. Everybody calls me "David the Daydreamer". You know why? Because I always daydream.

I daydream in my classes. I daydream in recess. I daydream at lunchtime. I daydream about adventures in jungles and deserts and under the ocean. It's fun, but I don't get good grades at school.

On Monday my mom said to me, "Go to the store and buy some bread." She gave me some money and I walked to the store. I started daydreaming. This is what I thought …

"I'm in the circus. There are lions and elephants and tigers and clowns. The clowns are jumping. The lions and tigers are running. People are riding on the elephants. The music is very loud. It's a very good circus."

I got to the store.

"What do you want, sonny?" said the store clerk.

"I don't know," I said. "I can't remember. It begins with 'b'."

"Some bananas?" said the store clerk.

"No, I don't like bananas."

"Some butter?" said the store clerk.

"I'm sorry," I said. "I can't remember."

The store clerk laughed. "Butter begins with 'b'," he said. "I think you want some butter."

So I got some butter.

In the street I started daydreaming. This is what I thought ...

"I'm in the jungle. There are tall trees and big flowers and butterflies. In the river, there are crocodiles. The crocodiles are looking at me. There's a big snake in the tree, and it's looking at me. There's a scorpion, and it's looking at me. It's very hot. The jungle is an amazing place ..."

I got home and I gave the butter to my mom.

"David," said Mom. "I don't want any butter. I want some bread." Bread! Of course.

"I can go back to the store, Mom," I said.

My mom laughed. "No, David," she said. "Don't worry."

"You have your head in the clouds," said Dad. He laughed.

"What are we going to do with you, David the Daydreamer?" asked Mom.

On Tuesday my friend Michael invited me to his house. He lives on the next street. I can walk to his house. I put my coat on.

"Goodbye, Mom!" I said. "I'm going to Michael's house."

"Have a nice time," said Mom. "And don't forget where you're going!"

I laughed. "I know where I'm going, Mom," I said. "I'm going to Michael's house."

I went out into the street. Can you guess what happened next? That's right. I started dreaming.

This is what I thought …

"I'm in a big city. There are cars and buses and people. There are tall buildings and stores and restaurants. I'm in a big black limousine. I'm going to meet the President. I'm a very important person. When people in the street see me, they say, 'Look! There's David! He's a very important person!'"

It was a very nice dream!

I walked and I walked and I walked. Then I stopped. I was lost! I was a long way from my house. I was on a street called Ocean Drive. I was very frightened.

There was a phone booth on the corner of the street. I had some change in my pocket. I phoned my mom.

"Mom!" I said. "I'm lost! I'm on a street called Ocean Drive. Can you come and get me?"

My mom came in the car. We went home.

"David," said Dad, "Mom and I are worried about you. You daydream all day long. You don't know what you're doing."

"I'm sorry, Dad," I said. "I like daydreaming. I like thinking about crazy things."

"Don't daydream in the street," said Mom. She looked very serious. "It's dangerous."

"I'm sorry, Mom," I said.

"What are we going to do with you, David the Daydreamer?" asked Mom.

13

* decision 결정

Wednesday was a bad day. In the morning, I went to school. My school is close to my house. I can walk to school. I picked up my backpack and I said goodbye to my mom.

"Don't forget where you're going!" said Mom.

I laughed. "I know where I'm going, Mom," I said. "I'm going to school."

I went out into the street. I started walking to school. And then ... Yes, I started daydreaming.

14

This is what I thought …
"I'm diving under the ocean. There are fish and sharks and whales. I'm going down, down, down to the bottom of the sea. I can see an old ship at the bottom. I'm going down to the ship. The ship is very old. It's a pirate's ship, and there's a treasure chest in it. I'm going to find the treasure. I'm going to be rich!"

Suddenly, I was on the ground and there was a terrible pain in my leg. I looked up and I saw a car. A man got out of the car. He was very worried.

"Call an ambulance!" he shouted.

"What happened?" I asked.

"You walked into the street. You walked into my car."

"My leg hurts," I said.

"Don't worry!" said the man. "We're going to take you to the hospital."

I was at home for two weeks. My leg was broken. It hurt a lot! I sat in my bedroom and I thought a lot. Here are some of the things I thought about ...

"I'm a famous movie star. Everybody wants my autograph!"

"I'm a chef in a restaurant. My food is delicious. The restaurant is full every night!"

"I'm an astronaut. I'm going to Mars. My rocket is landing on Mars. The Martians are coming to meet me!"

My father had a very good idea. He gave me a big notebook and he said, "Write a story."

I wrote one story, then I wrote another story, and another story …

I showed my stories to my dad and my mom and my brother. They all liked them. "Your stories are very good!" they said.

"You're a very clever boy!" my father said. "I really like your stories."

I was very happy!

Now I write stories every day. I don't daydream on the street now. When I get home, I sit down and write a story.

I write stories about the jungle. I write stories about the moon. I write stories about the desert and the ocean and people who do amazing things.

My family reads my stories. My friends read my stories. My teachers read my stories. Everyone likes my stories. One day I'm going to be a famous writer!

What are you good at?

Some people are good at math. They can add numbers and subtract numbers. They always get the right answer.

Some people are good at art. They can make beautiful pictures with pencils, crayons and paint. They can draw pictures of animals and houses and people.

Some people are good at sports. They can run and jump and swim very well. Sometimes they win medals in competitions.

Some people are good with animals. They like playing with animals. They like feeding animals. They like taking care of animals. They are happy when they are with animals.

Some people are good with computers. They always win computer games!

Some people are good at music. They can play the piano or the violin or the guitar. Everybody likes listening to their music.

Some people are good at thinking. They sit in a chair and they think. They think about adventures. They think about funny things. They think about sad things and happy things. Sometimes they write stories.

21

Everyone is good at something! You can be good at …

making cakes and cookies,

riding a bicycle,

telling jokes,

helping at home,

helping at school,

singing,

dancing,

flying a kite,

making people happy,

talking,

roller-skating,

looking after plants,

skateboarding,

making models,

or helping your friends.

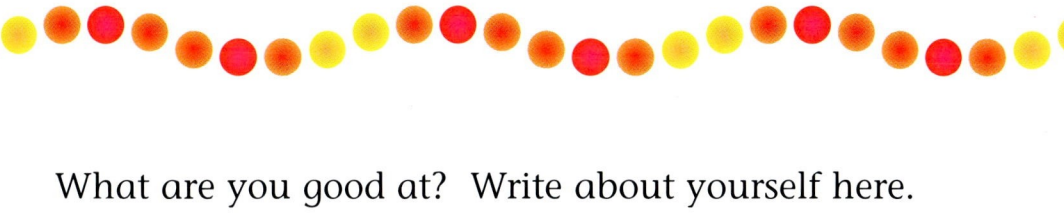

What are you good at? Write about yourself here.

_____
_____
_____
_____
_____
_____

Draw a picture of
yourself here.

Write your name here.

_____

Congratulations! You're great!

Activities

1. Write four words for each place.

crocodile

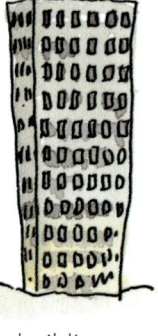

building

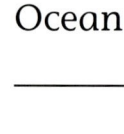

butterfly

shark

rocket

crab

Jungle
_____
_____
_____
_____

Ocean
_____
_____
_____
_____

City
_____
_____
_____
_____

Space
_____
_____
_____
_____

snake

planet

whale

car

star

parrot

store

spaceship

fish

bus

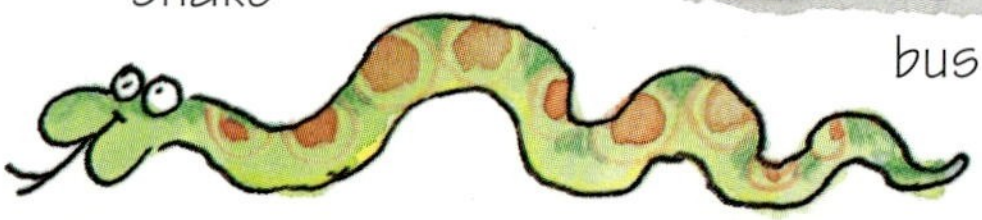

2. Help David write his shopping list. You can find 9 words in the square.

1. cilsnpe _____
2. nasbnaa _____
3. tebtur _____
4. derab _____
5. tenokoob _____
6. rycanos _____
7. sikooce _____
8. kcea _____
9. shfi _____
10. wsfoler _____

```
s  l  p  e  n  c  i  l  s
v  k  w  o  r  r  l  d  h
j  f  i  s  h  a  c  e  a
n  l  e  e  t  y  o  e  b
n  o  t  e  b  o  o  k  u
h  w  a  x  r  n  k  y  t
v  e  q  c  z  s  i  p  t
b  r  e  a  d  t  e  x  e
e  s  f  k  u  i  s  g  r
z  p  w  e  q  m  a  l  k
```

Which word is missing?

_____

25

3. **What a dream! Read and color.**

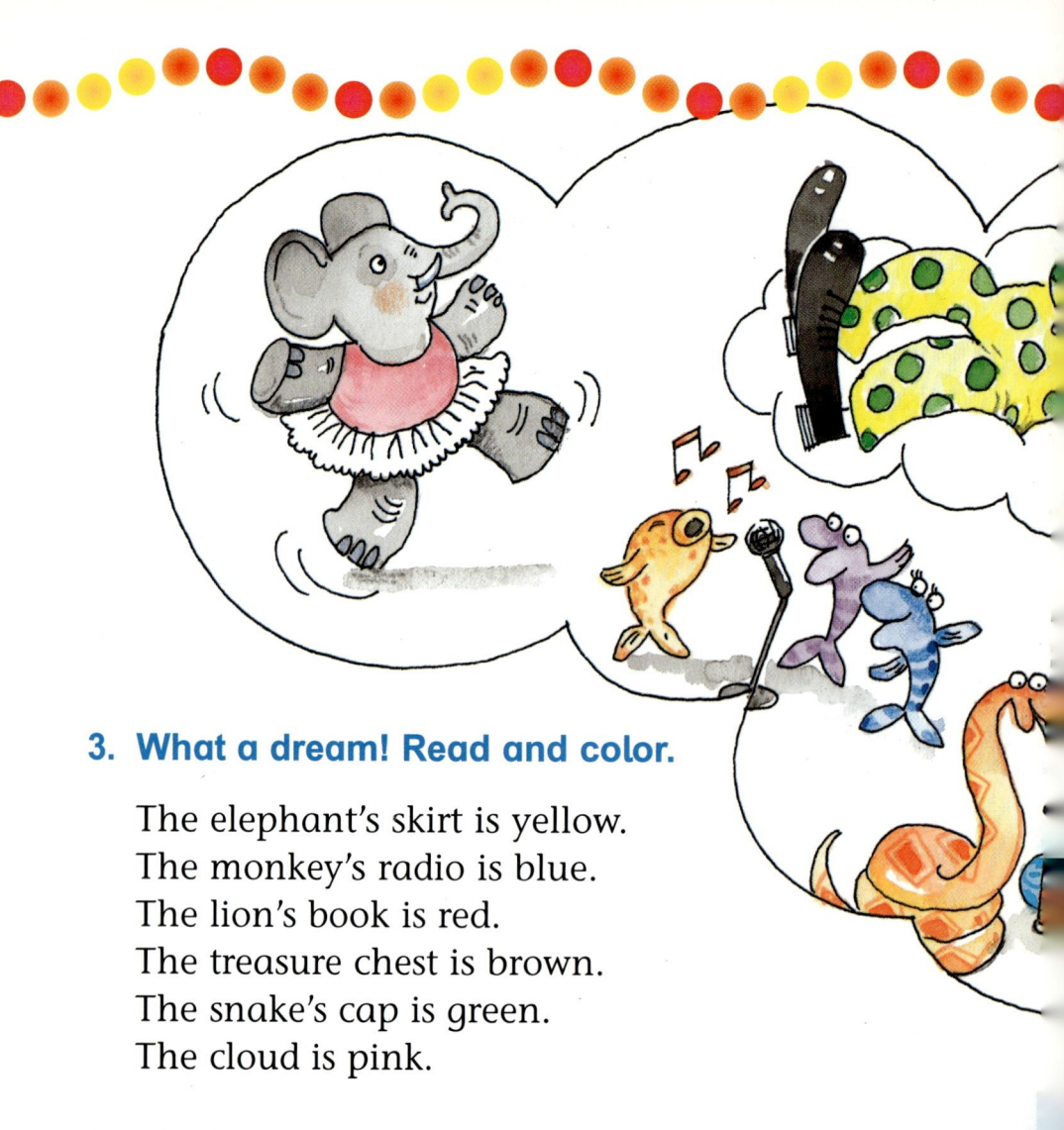

   The elephant's skirt is yellow.
   The monkey's radio is blue.
   The lion's book is red.
   The treasure chest is brown.
   The snake's cap is green.
   The cloud is pink.

4. **Find the mistakes.**

   The lion is listening to the radio.
   The snakes are eating sandwiches.
   The clown is singing.
   The fish are sleeping.
   The monkey is dancing.

Study the picture for a minute. Look at page 28.

Can you answer the questions?

27

5. Answer the questions. Don't look at the picture.

How many fish are there?

What color is the lion's book?

What is the elephant doing?

What are the snakes doing?

Where is the clown?

Is the lion sleeping?

Are the fish singing?

6. Write questions about the picture.

How many _____ ?

What color _____ ?

What is _____ ?

What are _____ ?

Where _____ ?

Is _____ ?

Are _____ ?

Ask your questions to your friends.

7. Crazy Futures! Choose numbers and discover your future!

Start

What are you going to be?
I'm going to be. . .

1   2   3   4

- a musician
- a movie star
- an astronaut
- an inventor

Where are you going to live?
I'm going to live in . . .

5   6   7   8

- the desert
- a small town
- a big city
- the jungle

What are you going to do?
I'm going to . . .

10   11   12

- meet important people
- invent a flying car
- visit all the planets
- discover treasure

It's going to be great!

Interview your friends!

Word List

a add
adventure
amazing

ambulance

astronaut
autograph

b

backpack

bananas
building
butter

c

chef

circus
clap
clown
cloud
competition
concert
crocodile

d dangerous
daydreamer
delicious
desert

diving

e elephant
f famous
frightened

g grades

guitar

h hospital
i important
inventor
j joke
jungle
l limousine
lion

m machine

math

medal

moon
movie star
musician

n notebook

p pattern

phone booth

piano
pirate
planet

r recess

s scorpion

serious
shark
ship
snake
subtract

t tiger

treasure chest

v violin

w whale

worried
writer

31

Macmillan Heinemann English Language Teaching
Between Towns Road, Oxford OX4 3PP, UK
A division of Macmillan Publishers Limited
Companies and representatives throughout the world

ISBN 0 333 71334 6

Text © Nick Beare and Jeanette Greenwell
Design and illustration © Macmillan Publishers Limited 1998
Heinemann is a registered trademark of Reed Educational and Professional Publishing Limited

First published 1988

All rights reserved; no part of this publication may be
reproduced, stored in a retrieval system, transmitted in any
form, or by any means, electronic, mechanical, photocopying,
recording, or otherwise, without the prior written permission
of the publishers.

Designed by StoreyBooks
Illustrations by Paula Martyr/Linden Artists Ltd
Cover illustration by Paula Martyr/Linden Artists Ltd

Printed in Hong Kong

2004   2003   2002   2001   2000
9   8   7   6   5   4   3